**FULL FLIGHT**
Beverley Grammar
School Library

Contents

Badger
L E A R N I N G

Why?

Why walk when you can run?

Why talk when you can shout?

Why pass when you can shoot?

Why wait in line when you can push to the front?

Why do your homework when you can watch telly?

Why go round the puddle when you can
jump right in it?

Why eat slowly when you can gobble it down?

Why go to bed when you can stay up and play?

Why eat vegetables when you can have sweets?

Why save your pocket money when you can spend it?

Why say 'please' and 'thank you' when you can
say 'yes' and 'no'?

Why?

Because adults have to have something to
say to children.

Ivor Baddiel

Computer Program to Turn Yourself into a Mermaid

Load Mirror.
Select Feet.
Ignore Error.
Press Delete.

Find Tail,
Copy, Paste.
Drag hair
Past waist.

Press Yes.
Program Saves
One mermaid.
Enter waves.

Celia Warren

The World's Greatest Goalie

I fly down the wing

Make a thunderous shot

Score a fabulous goal

That's the tenth I've got.

I love my mum

I love her a lot

But is she a great goalie?

I'm afraid she's not.

Roger Stevens

Monday Morning

Hot head, Mum tuts.

Into bed, no buts.

Fresh sheets, warm drink.

Want a treat, Mum winks.

Fake sleep, Mum goes.

Sneaky peep, tiptoes.

Channel flick, key turns.

Up quick! Mum returns.

Knocks twice. Here we go!

Choc-ice, Beano.

Head felt, asked how

Temperature normal now.

Later on practise cough.

(Radiator turned off.)

Rachel Rooney

The Pool

It was green and slimy and cool
As I dived headfirst in the pool
And the last thing I heard
Was the one single word
I think it might have been 'Fool'.

Dark and dank as I sank, sank, sank.

There were plants and rocks and a car
Which someone had driven too far
And then up popped a frog
From the smelly old bog
And I wished I'd remembered my jar!

Dark and dank as I sank, sank, sank.

An old boot came floating on by
With a sock, a shirt and a tie
They weren't quite my style
But I pondered a while
And thought that I'd give them a try.

Dark and dank as I sank, sank, sank.

By now I needed some air

As I swam past a conga eel's lair

And I no longer sank

As I reached for the bank

And a towel to dry off my hair.

Paul Nicholson

Advice to My Parents

Don't say *wicked*

Don't shout *cool*

No *High Fives*

When I walk in from school

Don't beam *fab*

Don't go *yeah*

Don't mouth *groovy*

Don't you dare!

In fact I think it's probably better

If you don't speak at all.

Jonny Zucker

Spooked

When your house feels strange
but you can't say why,
when you wake at night
to the echo of a cry.

When the floorboards creak
to the faintest footfall,
and the temperature drops
for no reason at all.

When the rocking chair rocks
but there's no one there,
when something has triggered
your squeaky stair.

When the curtains move
but there isn't a breeze,
when the house is empty
but you hear a sneeze...

You've been spooked by a spook,
now you're host to a ghost...

Brian Moses

It's Not That My Sister...

It's not that my sister's music annoys me.
I just can't stand the sound of it.

It's not that my sister's friends are bad-looking.
I just prefer not to look at their ugly faces.

It's not that my sister has a loud voice.
I just prefer to keep my door closed.

It's not that my sister is rude to me.
I just prefer to put my fingers in my ears.

It's not that my sister grasses me up.
I just prefer to get my excuses in first.

It's not that my sister lives in the same house as me.
I'd just prefer it if she moved.

Preferably to another planet.

Jonny Zucker

Football Dreaming

I'm
a striker racing,
a fullback chasing,
a winger crossing,
a captain bossing,
a wingback tackling,
a stopper shackling,
a halfback strolling,
a coach controlling,
a forward flicking,
a goalie kicking,
a linkman scheming,
a mad-fan dreaming
   on
      the
         morning
            bus
               to
                  school.

Wes Magee

Professor Plumcake's Wonderful Remote Control

Professor Plumcake's life-long goal
Was to invent the perfect
Remote control!

Press 1 if you want to turn on the lighting,
Press 2 to stop the kids from fighting,
Press 3 to tidy the bedroom floor,
Press 4 to open and shut the door,
Press 5 to rescue the cat from a tree,
Press 6 to make you a cup of tea,
Press 7 to cook you a tasty snack,
Press 8 to scratch your itchy back,
Press 9 to tuck you up safely in bed...

"I'm really fed up!"
The professor said.

I expect you're wondering
How that can be...

He's lost the remote control
Down the back of the settee!

David Orme

Dear Neighbours

We don't mind how loud you play
your rock and heavy metal,
even though it's turned so late;
gone ten, if not eleven.

We've got quite used to dog mess
every day outside our door;
if we can't share the joy of pets
then what are neighbours for?

We love to hang our washing out
to catch your bonfire smoke,
though barbecued pyjamas
would not suit every bloke.

But now it's time to let you know
we're moving house next week.
We would have called to tell you
But we know you never speak.

It's been a treat to know you,
we'll miss you – and your mess.
I'm sorry we can't leave you
a forwarding address...

Celia Warren

I Could Keep You All Behind After School

I could keep you all behind after school

I could make you write a thousand lines
I could make you do impossible sums
I could make you write up difficult experiments
I could make you learn really boring songs
I could make you spell massively long words
I could make you read a hundred pages.

I could keep you all behind after school

But I won't.

Because I want to go home.

Open Evening

I called their little darlings:
Awful
Nasty
Irritating
Mad
Annoying
Liars
Stupid
I was very *open* this evening.

Jonny Zucker

Am I in Love?

You're meant to hate girls
That's just the way it is
At our age.
But there's this one girl,
She's small and freckly with a really cute nose,
Who I just can't hate.
The others call her names,
Pull her hair,
And make faces at her,
But I just can't.
I can do it to her friends,
That's no problem,
But I've tried and tried to be horrible to her,
And I just can't.
Am I in love?

Ivor Baddiel

Stocking Surprise

Fishing socks
wind-up hen
money box and
torch pen.
Chocolate coin.
Don't know –
check it later.
Yes! I got a
Terminator.
Chocolate coin.
Harry Potter
magic set.
Look! I got a
Cyber Pet.
More chocolate
coins. One last
lump. Shake some
more. Orange
rolls out to
the floor. Tricked
again! Never
fear. Won't be
fooled again next year.

Rachel Rooney

Just Perfect

I'm not skilful enough for football
I'm not tall enough for basketball
I'm not handy enough for cricket
I'm not tough enough for rugby
I'm not springy enough for tennis
I'm not floaty enough for swimming
I'm not accurate enough for snooker
I'm not fast enough for athletics

I'm just perfect
For the sofa and remote control Olympics

Jonny Zucker

Canine Poem

Where do you get
Hot Dogs?

In sunny Berkshire.

Pie Corbett

The Goalie's Reasons

1. It wasn't fair, I wasn't ready...
2. Their striker was offside, it was obvious...
3. Phil got in my way, he always gets in my way, he should be dropped...
4. I had something in my eye...
5. I hadn't recovered from the last one that went in, or the one before that...
6. I thought I heard our head teacher calling my name...
7. Somebody exploded a blown-up crisp bag behind me...
8. There was a beetle on the pitch, I didn't want to tread on it...
9. Somebody exploded another crisp bag...
10. That girl was smiling at me, I don't like her doing that...
11. The goalposts must have been shifted, they weren't as wide before...
12. I thought I saw a UFO fly over the school...

And goal number 13?

It just wasn't a goal, I'm sorry, it just wasn't a goal and that's that. OK?

Brian Moses

Hallowe'en

Darren's got a pumpkin
Hollowed out a treat.
He put it in the window
It scared half the street.

I wish I had a pumpkin
But I've not and it's a shame
I've got a scary carrot
But it's not the same.

Roger Stevens

Toffee

He legged it out as fast as he could
'Cos he hadn't paid as really he should.
Faster and faster he ran down the street
Clutching the toffee but who did he meet?

"You seem in a hurry," said PC Tapper
As Billy quickly undid the wrapper.
"What are you up to young Billy Hill?"
"Not very much," Billy lied with skill.

"Any more toffees like the one you have there?"
"You can have this one," said Billy, "it's spare."
"Thanks very much, don't mind if I do,"
Drat it! Thought Billy, I wish I'd nicked two.

Then up came running, the man from the shop
"What's up with him?" asked the toffee-chewing cop.
But Billy had gone, he'd legged it once more,
With the adults left standing to work out the score.

Paul Nicholson

Song of the Martian Ghosts

Mars was a beautiful planet once,
Just like yours –
Forests and mountains,
Seas crashing on rocky shores,
And us   the Martians.
But our seas dried up,
Our forests died,
We couldn't stay alive,
However hard we tried –
And now we're just ghosts,
Whispering in the cold wind,
In the dark places under rocks,
Waiting for you to arrive.

Come quickly, you men –
For when
Your first silver ship lands,
And opens its doors,
We'll slip inside,
For that's our plan –
To hitch a ride
To your beautiful green planet in the sky,
Where it's warm and wet,
And we can live again.

And once we're there
You'll never get rid of us.
However hard you try.

David Orme

The Wembley Way

*(In memory of the old Wembley Stadium,
the home of football)*

One sunny Saturday in May
we joined the crowds on Wembley Way.

We joined the fans all walking up
to watch the final of the Cup.

We saw the banners held up high
and saw the flags against the sky.

The fans all joked and larked about,
and "*Wembley! Wembley!*" was the shout.

"*Come on you Blues!*" "*Come on you Reds!*"
We saw huge coloured hats on heads.

Both sets of fans let laughter ring
and you should just have heard them sing.

There was no nastiness, just fun
as all the fans smiled in the sun.

The game was great. Ten out of ten.
But nothing matched the friendship when

Up for the Cup on Final Day
we joined the crowds on Wembley Way.

Wes Magee

Dress Code

We're going to Aunty Bella's
My mum told me one Sunday evening.
Me and your dad are going there now
Join us there as soon as you're out of the bath.
And please wear something smart
Their children are always so neatly dressed.
Don't show us up
She begged me.

So I put on the smartest outfit
I could find.
Purple flares.
Multicoloured tie-dye grandpa shirt.
Massive Doc Martens.
Huge silver sunglasses.
And a great beaded chain round my neck saying *Chill out*.

As I pushed open Aunty Bella's front door
The sentence on my mum's lips,
Was in code.
Dress code.

And although I didn't understand a word of it,
I didn't much like the sound of it.

Jonny Zucker

Too Bad!

My shirt's too small
And my socks are holey,
But nobody cares,
I'm only the goalie.

Here come the Forwards
On the attack,
Where's our Defender?
Where's our Back?

It's all up to me
To stop the ball,
It's coming high and
I'm only small...

I did it. A save!
Only one slight hitch
I'm in the wrong goal
At the wrong end of the pitch!

Celia Warren

POEM

I am a poem,
P-O-E-M.
Sometimes I rhyme,
And keep to a certain time.
Then again,
Sometimes I don't.
Bit like a story,
Only shorter,
Which is fine by me,
'Cos I get read quickly.
See,
I'm over already.
I hope you enjoyed me.

Ivor Baddiel

Don't Move the Goal Posts

Don't move the goal posts.
Leave them as they are...

Well, maybe this much wider.
Now you've gone too far.

In a bit more. Stop.
OK, that'll do...

No! You can't wear your jumper
Unless you swap it for a shoe.

What do you mean you're cold now?
You always have to moan!

Don't go. I didn't mean it.
I can't play on my own.

Rachel Rooney

When Dad Went into Space

What was it like in space, dad?
You've seen the snaps, he said.
Like being in a church
Or rising from the dead.

The colours were much brighter
Louder and somehow scented.
To tell you properly I'd need words
That haven't been invented.

How's it feel to be back? I asked
Dad smiled and shed a tear.
The gravity – well, that's a drag
But I love the atmosphere.

Roger Stevens

The Christmas Meal

Grampa Bill
ate his fill
at the Christmas
table.

Sonny Jim
kept quite slim
and so did
Auntie Mabel.

Billy Bott
scoffed the lot,
whenever
he was able.

Terrence Telly
filled his belly,
according
to the fable

But Granma Stout
ate nowt!

Pie Corbett

Back to School

A week after the holiday begins
and there it is, in every shop window in town,
'Back to School' – I ask you.
As soon as they set us free,
the shops are all telling us
we've got to go back again.

I don't want new clothes,
I don't want new pencil cases,
I don't want new maths equipment,
I just want to be left alone,
I want to be on holiday
and not reminded how
in 4 weeks, 5 days, 7 hours, 39 minutes and 13 seconds
I'll be back at school.

And in one shop they even spelt it
'B-A-K'.
Well I reckon the people who wrote that sign
ought to go back to school too,
so they can learn to spell properly.
And here's what I say
to all those places that tell me
it's 'Back to School' –
'Back off – will you?'
'It's my holiday!'

Brian Moses

Stop Talking at the Back!

Lessons are for listening, Tom and Terry Mack
And while we're on the subject, stop talking at the back!
If Mrs Thomas hears this noise, I'm sure I'll get the sack
And while we're on the subject, stop talking at the back!

Stop whispering your nonsense, Bella, Paul and Jack
And while we're on the subject, stop talking at the back!
I see my theme is lost on you, I'll have to change my tack
And while we're on the subject, stop talking at the back!

Other teachers keep control, I'll have to face their flack
And while we're on the subject, stop talking at the back!

Mrs Thomas, how nice to see you, what is that you say?
You were outside in the playground
and chose to walk this way
You're sure you heard an awful din
and thought I'd lost my track?
No everyone's been good as gold, especially at the back.

Jonny Zucker

Titles in Full Flight Impact

The Bombed House	Jonny Zucker
Gang of Fire	Jonny Zucker
Big Brother @ School	Jillian Powell
Rollercoaster	Jillian Powell
Monster Planet	David Orme
Danger Mountain	David Orme
Goal Scorers	Jonny Zucker
Basketball	Tony Norman
Fight to the Death! A Play	Stan Cullimore
Stop Talking at the Back and other poems	(ed.) Jonny Zucker

Badger Publishing Limited
Oldmedow Road, Hardwick Industrial Estate, King's Lynn PE30 4JJ
Telephone: 01438 791037
www.badgerlearning.co.uk

2 4 6 8 10 9 7 5 3 1

Stop Talking at the Back and other poems ISBN 978 1 85880 387 6

First edition © 2003
This second edition © 2013

Series Editor: Jonny Zucker.   Editor: Paul Martin.
Cover design: Jain Birchenough.   Cover illustration: Paul Savage.
Publisher: David Jamieson.